START-UP
SCIENCE
HEALTH AND GROWTH

Claire Llewellyn

Evans

Published by Evans Brothers Limited
2A Portman Mansions
Chiltern Street
London W1U 6NR

© Evans Brothers Limited 2004
Reprinted 2005
Produced for Evans Brothers Limited by
White-Thomson Publishing Ltd.
2/3 St Andrew's Place
Lewes, East Sussex BN7 1UP

Printed in China by WKT Company Limited

Editor: Dereen Taylor
Consultants: Les Jones, Science Consultant, Manchester
Education Partnership; Norah Granger, former primary
headteacher and senior lecturer in education, University
of Brighton
Designer: Leishman Design
Artwork page 9: Tom Price, age 7

Cover: All photographs by Chris Fairclough.

British Library Cataloguing in Publication Data
Llewellyn, Claire
   Health and growth - (Start-up science)
   1.Growth - Juvenile literature 2. Health - Juvenile
literature
   I.Title
   571.8

ISBN: 0 237 526441

Acknowledgements:
Special thanks to the following for their help and
involvement in the preparation of this book: Staff and
pupils at Elm Grove Primary School, Brighton, Liz Price
and family and friends, Christine Clark and family
and friends.

Picture Acknowledgements:
Chris Fairclough Colour Library 7 *(top middle, bottom
right);* 8 *(top left);* Ecoscene 7 *(top left, top right, bottom
left, bottom middle);* Shailen Patel 5 *(middle, bottom left).*
All other photographs by Chris Fairclough.

Contents

A new baby

▼ Joseph has a baby brother called Jack. Jack is only 12 weeks old. Joseph's mum and dad care for Jack.

▲ They feed him, wash him and change his nappy. They comfort him when he cries.

baby care feed wash change

▶ Joseph is three years old. He can build a tower with bricks. What other things can Joseph do that baby Jack can't?

▶ Shailen, 6 years old

◀ Shailen, 6 months old

Find photos of you when you were a baby. How have you changed?

nappy comfort years months 5

Growing older

Babies grow quickly. Week by week, they grow bigger and stronger. Before their first birthday, they can move around and begin to feed themselves.

Year by year, children grow bigger and learn to do more by themselves. Children grow up into adults.

grow   week   bigger   stronger

Many baby animals are cared for by their parents. When they have grown into adults, they have babies of their own.

Look at the animals in these pictures. Which baby belongs to which adult?

birthday   adults   animals   parents

Food for life

All humans and animals need food to grow and stay alive. Without food and water they would die.

Most of us eat three meals a day. At the end of each meal, we feel 'full up' but we soon get hungry again.

▶ Today, Tom has made a list of everything he has had to eat and drink.

He has made a chart of the different foods and drinks.

food alive water die

What have you eaten and drunk today? What would be on your chart?

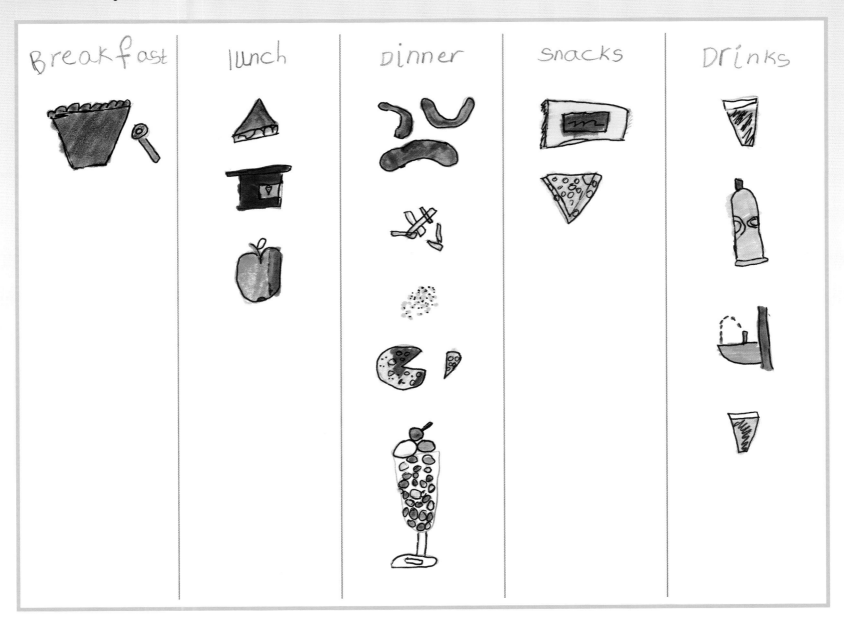

Breakfast	lunch	Dinner	snacks	Drinks

meals hungry drinks

Looking at foods

There are many different kinds of food. They help our bodies in different ways.

▶ Foods like bread, potatoes and pasta help to give us energy.

◀ Foods like meat, fish and eggs help to build our bodies. Vegetarians may eat beans and pulses instead of meat and fish.

bodies energy build vegetarians

◀ **Foods like apples, oranges and courgettes help to keep us fit and healthy.**

We need to eat foods from all of these groups to grow and keep our bodies healthy.

▲ **Which group does each food belong to?**

fit   healthy   groups

Favourite foods

Today is Alex's birthday. He is having a chocolate birthday cake. Chocolate is Alex's favourite food. He doesn't eat it every day. This is a special treat.

What are your favourite foods?
What would you like to eat at your birthday party?

chocolate cake favourite

Alex asks his friends what their favourite foods are.

I love strawberry milkshake. It's sweet and creamy.

Mmm! Crisps are really crunchy.

My favourite is pepperoni pizza. It's spicy.

special treat   strawberry   pizza   13

Food words

There are many different words to **describe** foods.

glistening brown long fat

▲ **Some words describe the way a food looks.**

sweet tangy sharp sour

▲ **Some words describe the way it tastes.**

▶ **Other words describe the way food feels.**

slippery smooth soft stringy

describe looks

▼ **Look at the foods in these pictures.**

sweet cold slippery fruity

crisp juicy crunchy dry creamy

Which words would you choose to describe each food?

tastes   feels

Let's exercise!

Morrissey is running after a football. Lizzie is climbing on a climbing frame.

Which parts of their bodies are working hard?

Working our bodies helps us to stay healthy. It makes us stronger, too.

running climbing working

Exercise is very good for us.

▼ **How do you feel before you exercise?**

▼ **How do you feel when you exercise?**

An exercise pictogram

► Gita asked children in her class what exercise they do out of school.

▲ She typed in all the information...

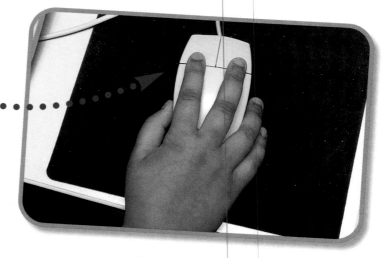

▲ ...and used the mouse to draw a pictogram.

pictogram walking cycling

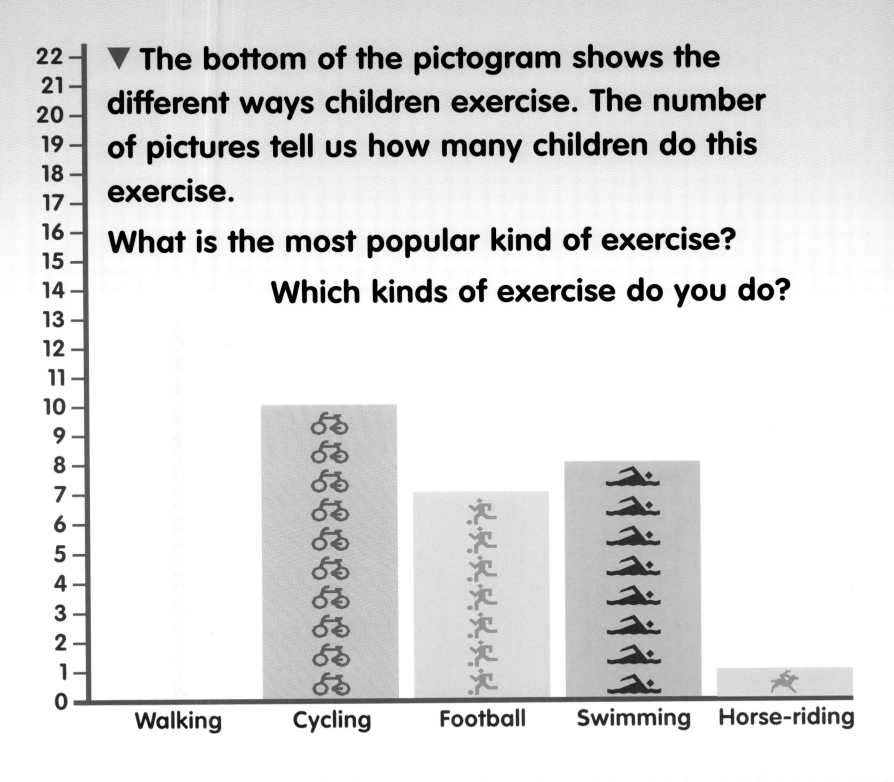

▼ The bottom of the pictogram shows the different ways children exercise. The number of pictures tell us how many children do this exercise.

What is the most popular kind of exercise?

Which kinds of exercise do you do?

football swimming horse-riding 19

Feeling ill

▼ **Rosie is feeling ill today. She is hot and very tired.**

▲ **The doctor has given Rosie's mum some medicine. This will help to make Rosie better.**

The medicine is very strong. Rosie only needs a small dose.

ill   doctor   medicine   dose

⚡ WARNING!

Medicines can be dangerous. Never take medicine without asking an adult first.

▼ The packaging of sweets and medicines sometimes looks the same.

Are you sure that you could pick out the sweets and not choose the medicines by mistake?

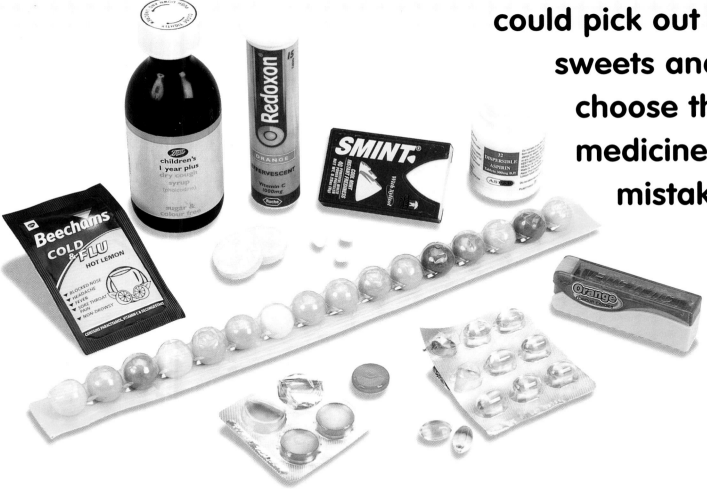

dangerous   packaging

Further information for

New words listed in the text:

			energy	healthy	packaging	tastes
			favourite	horse-riding	parents	vegetarians
adults	build	cycling	feed	hungry	pictogram	walking
alive	cake	dangerous	feels	ill	pizza	wash
animals	care	describe	fit	looks	running	water
baby	change	die	food	meals	special treat	week
bigger	chocolate	doctor	football	medicine	strawberry	working
birthday	climbing	dose	groups	months	stronger	years
bodies	comfort	drinks	grow	nappy	swimming	

Possible Activities

PAGES 4-5
Ask children to bring in a photo of themselves as babies and make a wall display. Can the children guess who the babies are?

PAGES 6-7
Collect and label pictures of animals and their young. Discuss the special names that we give to young animals (e.g. calf, cub, piglet, etc).

Observe young animals first-hand at a farm. Some children may have young pets that might be brought into school.

Discuss the things children can do now that they couldn't do one or more years ago. What new things are they keen to do when they are older?

PAGES 8-9
Draw a food diary for a day. How many different foods are there?

Ask children to make a note of what they drink in a day. How much do they drink? Use the results to make a chart.

PAGES 10-11
Have a fruit tasting day. Ask all the children to bring in a piece of fruit, ensuring as wide a range as possible. Chop up the fruit to make a huge fruit salad that everyone can share.

Visit a supermarket to see how many different foods are available. How many different kinds of pasta, apples and juices can they find?

PAGES 12-13
Do a survey to find out the children's favourite foods. Turn your results into a chart/pictogram.

Make a class display of a dream birthday party. What food and drink would the children include?

Parents and Teachers

PAGES 14-15

Collect pictures that could be the starting point for literacy work about different foods (e.g. raw carrots, tomatoes, hot soup). Make a list of words to suit each food. Can children guess the food from the words?

Write advertisements for different foods – e.g. Buy these apples, they're crunchy and sweet – and use them to make a display.

Read some poems about food. Ask the children to try writing their own.

PAGES 16-17

Take the children for a run round the playground. Ask them how they feel before and after the run. Do they notice any changes in their body?

PAGES 18-19

Conduct a survey of the exercise children do. Create a pictogram for your class.

Develop a simple playground game that gives players plenty of exercise at break time. Use a ball and running, jumping, skipping or other vigorous activity.

PAGES 20-21

Discuss with children how they feel when they are ill. How does it feel to get better again?

Discuss the dangers associated with medicines and draw a picture showing where medicines should be stored at home. Show the children medicine containers with special child-proof lids and discuss why these are used.

Further Information

BOOKS FOR CHILDREN

Am I Fit and Healthy? by Claire Llewellyn (Hodder Wayland, 1999)

How Do They Grow? series by Jillian Powell (Hodder Wayland, 2001)

Let's Explore: Keeping Healthy/Babies/Growing Up by Henry Pluckrose (Franklin Watts, 2003)

Look After Yourself: Your Body/Your Food by Claire Llewellyn (Franklin Watts, 2002)

My Healthy Body: Eating/Fit and Well by Veronica Ross (Belitha Press, 2002)

Watch it Grow series by Barrie Watts (Franklin Watts, 2003)

Why Can't I Eat Just Sweets? by Ruth Thomson (Belitha Press, 2002)

WEBSITES

www.bbc.co.uk/health/kids/
www.kidshealth.org/kid/
www.kidshealth.org/parent/nutrition_fit/nutrition/vegetarianism
www.primaryresources.co.uk/science

Index